FOLLOW, LEAD, BUILD.

THE ULTIMATE GUIDE TO NETWORK MARKETING

Raymond Young

Produced by:

FriesenPress
Suite 300 – 852 Fort Street
Victoria, BC, Canada V8W 1H8

www.friesenpress.com

Distributed to the trade by The Ingram Book Company

This book has been given to: _____

If you have questions, contact: _____

Foreword

MJ Durkin

Author, Speaker and Creator of Recommendation Selling™

If you are thinking about starting your own business in relationship marketing or direct selling, or you have already joined forces with a company that you believe in, you need to read this book! Actually, I'm going to recommend that you study it, underline it, highlight it, and read several pages a day for the next 90 days. Yes, re-read the book several times, because there are few books on the market today that will help you succeed in relationship-marketing, or direct selling, as much as this one will.

Ray Young and I teamed up several years ago. Ray would bring me in, at least twice a year, to train large audiences of his partners and representatives on the finer aspects of prospecting, presenting, and closing deals. Ray and I always hit it off, and seemed to understand each other as it related to building a business. After reading *"Follow, Lead, Build – The Ultimate Guide to Network Marketing,"* I finally understood why.

Ray's conceptual understanding of what a new person goes through, when they first join a relationship-marketing company, is only enhanced by the fact that he's actually gone through the same things and survived! Not only did he survive the disbelief and non-supportive actions of his friends, but also went on to thrive and become one of the top income earners in North America, in the relationship-marketing and direct selling industry. Ray Young knows what he's talking about when he's discussing how to be successful in this industry, because he's been on the front lines, *Following, Leading* and *Building!* He built one of the fastest growing and most profitable organizations that I have ever seen. Ray's "famous" Wednesday morning meeting was one of the most amazing "weekly trainings" I have ever witnessed. Who else in relationship-marketing could put 200 to 300 people in a room every single week, for *years*? There aren't that many leaders who could pull that off consistently. Using the same principles as those in this book, Ray was able to help large numbers of people make money, stay motivated, and enhance their lives. This is why I highly recommend that you read this book—no, study it—like your financial life depends on it, because it probably does!

From the first chapter, in which you'll learn that you should be extremely careful about whom you listen to, right up to the last chapter, in which you'll get a glimpse of what is possible for you if you choose to *Follow, Lead and Build*—the author will give you all of the belief systems you will need to be successful. Take this book seriously. It will help you. I highly recommend it!

Introduction

The purpose of this book is to help as many people as possible achieve their goals, and dreams, through their own network marketing or home-based business. You have, most likely, just entered the world of network marketing for the first time, and have very little information about what to do next. Rest assured of two things: You have a team that wants to see you succeed; and, if you follow the fundamentals outlined in this book, you will increase your chances of achieving your goals without making the common mistakes most people make when joining a new network marketing company for the first time. I am excited to share with you my 30 years of experience in building and developing businesses, which has allowed me the luxury of not having to work for anyone or depend on a job as my only source of income. I am a huge proponent of freedom … particularly financial freedom. True freedom is the ability to choose what you do with your time, with whom you choose to do it, and for how long you choose to do it. My goal is to help you obtain this type of freedom.

I am certain that the topics and lessons in this book will benefit anyone who has recently joined a network marketing business of some kind, one with a product or service that is attractive enough to get you involved. Many people will quickly realize that simply wishing for your dreams in life will not help you to achieve them, nor will just getting involved in something guarantee success. It is the goal of this book to accomplish two key things: identify the natural fears and negative attitudes that you may encounter when attempting something outside of your natural existence, and help you to develop the skills needed to tune-out anything that is holding you back from true success. It will also give you the tools you need to develop your leadership ability to the point where success in your chosen business is not only possible, but probable.

I will help you to develop your confidence, people skills, and leadership qualities so that, whether you are looking at becoming involved in a business opportunity or just want to be the best version of yourself that you can be, you will be better equipped to move forward.

Over the past 30 years, I have built businesses in three completely different markets and industries. I began my entrepreneurial journey as a concert promoter. In fact, I was one of the youngest independent concert promoters, starting at the age of 16. I built my business into an entertainment company that included live entertainment services, disc jockey services, and sound and lighting services. This was the initial eye-opener that made me realize that doing something for <u>yourself</u> is far better than doing it for someone else.

When I was 20 years old, I entered the gas/service station business. By the time I was 21, I had become the largest independent owner/operator in my district, with five outlets in my name. By the age of 25, I had already purchased five rental properties and had continued to build my business by adding other components, such as truck rentals, a limousine business, and other sales and marketing products. By most people's measure of success, I was doing great.

Over this 13-year period as a successful entrepreneur, I constantly entertained opportunities in the network marketing world and, when I left the gas station business, I made the decision to commit full-time to network marketing.

As I will describe in this book, network marketing is the most cost-effective way to build a business that creates residual financial income, freedom, and total financial independence. My primary purpose in writing it is to address all the important issues regarding the building of a successful network marketing organization—and the successes and failures I have witnessed on my journey.

Over a 16-year period with my chosen network marketing company, I broke (and then held) company records for the most production and income in a single month, and maintained one of the largest recruiting and production teams for almost a decade. I will explain to you the changes I went through, personally, in order to make that happen: the steps I followed on a daily, weekly, and monthly basis, and the disciplines that ensured my success. I will clearly describe the person you will want to become in order to make the same results happen for you. I want to teach you that, once a decision has been made and an effective plan is put into action, recognition and rewards inevitably follow.

As we head into the meat and potatoes of success and failure in network marketing, I want you to know this: I am just like you. From a very young age, all I ever wanted was a chance to be somebody. I wanted to make my family proud. I wanted to do something great with my life, to be someone great and have a positive and profound impact on the people around me. I was lucky, in that I *knew* I had the drive and the ambition, as well as the desire ... I just needed the right vehicle. Network marketing was that vehicle for me, as it can be for you.

As a side note, I want to mention that everything I accomplished, I did even though I never made it through high school. While I am certainly not advocating that route, I wanted to point out that an obstacle that could have held me back, or held me down, did not. We all have obstacles in our lives. The trick is to never let them stop you.

Thanks to my parents, I learned important values, and a strong work ethic. I always did what I said I was going to do, and never expected anything for free. At a young age, I learned from my father that, "things don't happen, people *make* things happen."

When you are finished this book, and apply the principles within it, you will be a person able to *make* things happen for you and your family, in ways you never knew were possible.

Chapter One

What Have I Just Joined?

When first recruited into a new business venture, most people experience a multitude of emotions. They are typically incredibly excited about their new opportunity and their future. They may also experience a measure of anxiety, worry, doubt, and fear about their skills and abilities. They may feel confused. However, something has inspired them to set aside those feelings and get involved in a business, for which they most likely have no experience or education. The reason, I believe, is that everyone wants a chance to have more. Is that not why you have seized opportunities presented to you? No doubt it is. Regardless of a person's current position and status in life, one characteristic that all people share in common is an innate desire to do better, to improve, to achieve more.

Unfortunately, getting "more" rarely happens the easy way … without our having to work hard to get it. For example, very few will become wealthy by simply winning a lottery, or receiving an inheritance. The reality is, if one of those things were to happen to you, the money would likely not last very long.

Financial freedom that isn't earned through hard work tends not to be appreciated and so becomes temporary.

There are no greater victories in life than the ones you create yourself, and are able to take responsibility for. And, more than likely, you have chosen, or will choose, to start a new business venture in order to acquire "more" and gain your financial freedom. However, I would ask you to understand one thing: *freedom is not free*. Freedom comes with its own price tag. True freedom requires commitment, sacrifice, an investment of your time—days, evenings, and weekends—and a dedication to constant and never-ending self-improvement. This is one of my favorite sentences: Victory is sweet when the price is great! Don't shy away from the price! Pay the price, enjoy the journey, stay the course ... and when freedom is yours, you will know it was worth it.

The title of this chapter is: "What have I just joined?"

Network marketing, word-of-mouth marketing, interactive distribution, and relationship marketing all share common elements in that the companies bypass traditional media-based marketing (print, radio, or TV) and instead rely on their independent sales-force (or distributors) marketing their product or services to their own personal and professional networks. The salesperson is compensated through a sales margin, and sometimes through the ability to "override" the sales efforts of other salespeople whom they recruit into the same model.

The upfront benefits of low start-up costs, relaxed qualifications, and flexible working hours make these networking marketing programs attractive to anyone looking for part-time income to supplement an existing career, or as a new career for full-time income.

I have to say that, in the last 16 years, I have heard all sorts of criticisms of this kind of company, some truly ridiculous. For example, you may have heard people describe the network marketing business model as a scam, pyramid, or cult. Let's look at these terms and accusations individually.

SCAM: "a dishonest scheme; a fraud" - Oxford American Dictionaries

Could you really be joining a scam? Well, if the company you have joined is publicly traded, or at least licensed with a government agency to allow it to do business, the answer is no. So why do so many people automatically consider any network marketing opportunity to be a scam?

The answer is simple. People are afraid of things they don't understand, and the friends and family of people choosing to venture into unfamiliar opportunities are no different. How does an average and ordinary person get the chance to excel, achieve, and possibly make hundreds of thousands of dollars?

"It's too good to be true."

"They're just after your money."

People you thought were your friends might even say things like: "You're not smart enough to do that" or ask, "What makes you think that you're good enough to do that?"

The truth is, the world is full of naysayers and skeptics. Just because one of your friends or family members suggests that you are being taken advantage of, it does not mean that you are. Do your homework, check out the credentials, and then trust in what you have learned, and don't let anyone else's fear make you doubt what you know to be true or right.

Truth be told, calling a business opportunity a scam is something of a cop-out. It is one of those sarcastic remarks that are typically stated as fact, without any measure of proof. When faced with that assumption, I recommend responding with something like this:

"No kidding? I wasn't aware of that. My research into the company hasn't shown me anything of the sort. Please, tell me what you've heard or read that has given you the impression that this business is a scam?"

You will be pleasantly surprised when there is no valid response.

The "too good to be true" phrase is also thrown around quite freely when describing network marketing opportunities. When you consider what it is actually saying, it also seems to be a rather poor excuse for a reasonable argument. Think back on your very first job, probably working part-time, and for minimum wage. Then consider your current income. At that starting point in your life, making whatever it is your making now, be it $20,000 or $50,000, would undoubtedly have seemed too good to be true. You know it isn't, but perception is a funny thing, and always subject to change. Your perception is your reality at any moment in time.

I felt the same way when I was introduced to a leader in the network marketing business, which I had joined, who had just taken his income through $500,000 annually. Sure, I wanted to make that kind of money, but the words "too good to be true" certainly went through my mind. Obviously, when my income surpassed that milestone, I no longer felt the same way. The income potential of your opportunity will only seem too good to be true until you reach it.

According to the Federal Trade Commission in the US, and Industry Canada in Canada, network marketing companies are legitimate businesses that may freely operate in all US states and Canadian provinces.

PYRAMID: "a system of financial growth achieved by a small initial investment, with subsequent investments being funded by using unrealized profits as collateral." - Oxford American Dictionaries

Although the company you have joined, or are considering joining, may have a pyramid-like structure, it is probably *not* an illegal pyramid scheme. The fact that you have to make money from the efforts of others does not make it a pyramid. If that were the case, all companies with employees and salespeople would fit this description. Unless you are forced to invest money for no product, no service, no licensing, and no true value, and ask your friends and family to do the same, you have *not* joined a pyramid.

The cost to join your network marketing company should be, and generally is, in direct proportion to the *initial value being provided by said company*—a very small investment in comparison to the potential return on capital to be gained if you follow your leaders' advice and your company's system.

Once again, if someone presents you with this objection to your involvement in a new business venture, ask for clarification. I find the obvious question to ask is: "A pyramid? What do you mean by that?"

First, be sure that anyone who would use the word pyramid in an insulting manner is likely repeating something they have heard, and will not be able to substantiate it. If I asked you to define a pyramid, could you accurately do so? More often than not, you will hear something to do with getting paid on the efforts of other people.

This is NOT the definition of a pyramid. This is Business 101. I have never been shy about setting the record straight when people say things that are inaccurate.

"Based on your definition," I respond, "any business that makes its living via the efforts of salespeople is a pyramid. Is that right? So all real estate companies are pyramids then? All investment firms? All car dealerships? They all have owners and brokers who make a profit from the efforts of other people ... so are they all pyramids too?"

So, while pyramids-schemes may share a similar physical structure to some network marketing and relationship marketing business models, I hope it is now clear that there are fundamental differences as well. You should now be able to look, with understanding and clarity, at what you have joined, or are thinking about joining, and see plainly that is not a pyramid, or a scam, but falls instead under the same business model as most companies – with products or services being brought to the consumer by way of a marketing system, of which people are a part.

If this topic interests you, please check with government agencies in your area. The Federal Trade Commission in the US, and Industry Canada in Canada, are very clear on what constitutes a pyramid, and are quick to label pyramids as illegal. Typical criteria for an illegal pyramid include:

- Participants pay money for the right to receive compensation for recruiting
- A participant is required to buy a specific quantity of products, other than at cost price for the purpose of advertising, before they are allowed to join the plan or advance within the plan
- Participants are knowingly sold commercially unreasonable quantities of the product or products (a practice known as "inventory loading")
- Participants are not allowed to return products on reasonable commercial terms

Providing your company does not break these basic rules, you have not joined a pyramid, and can represent your company and build your business with confidence.

CULT:"a relatively small group of people having religious beliefs or practices regarded by others as strange or sinister" - Oxford American Dictionaries

This is my favorite. "Cult" is derived from the word "culture". I always loved when people called me and accused me of trying to recruit their family members into a cult. It never ceased to entertain me. Understand that a cult is merely a group of like-minded people, working together with like-minded ideas. Based on those criteria, you could consider the largest part of the population in North America to be a cult. The middle class is the largest group of people in history to be completely and totally like-minded in their lifestyle patterns.

For example, the middle class will generally spend money they don't have, on things they don't need and cannot afford. Worst of all, they fool themselves into thinking that they *can* afford it and that they need it!

Over the past 30 years, I have experienced poverty, middle class, and wealth. I am sure I could spend the better part of this book giving you examples of how the middle class have been manipulated, and directed how to think, by the government and the media. The worst part is that nobody wants to recognize that we have all been fooled into settling for what somebody told us we are worth. Maybe now is your opportunity to be a part of a culture that focuses on winning and having more, and that offers the opportunity to rise above the normal middle class way of thinking.

After reviewing the above negative impressions and descriptions, which you may hear regarding your new business opportunity, you will hopefully agree that such comments are generally shared with a lack of knowledge and understanding. I am sure you will also agree that focusing on such negativity will only take away from your success and your ability to become someone truly special.

However, should anyone feel the need to share such a comment with you, you now have the necessary information with which to educate them, about the legitimacy of your chosen company.

As your belief in your company and your own business grows, and as you begin to experience success, two amazing things *will* begin to happen:

First, your belief and confidence will become apparent to everyone you come into contact with. For this reason, I work very hard at ensuring that my people are very good at handling questions and objections. I do this so that they can have the confidence to begin conversations anytime and anywhere, without fear of the occasional objection being raised. You will find that you must endure far less negativity from friends, family, and prospects once you have reached a level of competency in handling questions and objections. People seem to sense when you know your business well. Case in point, when presenting my business to a new person or a group of people, I truly look forward to handling their objections. More often than not, no objections or concerns are raised. Your confidence will become so obvious to everyone that only the most important issues will be brought to your attention.

Secondly, if you *do* receive negative feedback from friends, family, and prospects, you will find that their comments will have far less impact on you. Once you are experiencing success, it becomes very easy to shrug off comments from anyone you believe is speaking from a place of ignorance. You will begin to understand that such an individual simply has no clue, and that you already know far more than they do. You will have acquired the ability and courage to break away from naysayers and negative people, and all the things that have always held you back in life.

It must be said that no one, myself included, enjoys negative comments, sarcasm, or criticism. It is especially tough to take when the giver is a close friend or a family member. Even worse, if you've done your due diligence and researched a company and product/service, and you believe wholeheartedly in them, you may not even understand where the negativity is coming from. You see the truth ... why can't they? Unquestionably, balancing your love, respect, and admiration for the same people who would criticize your decision to go into business for yourself is one of the most difficult obstacles to tackle in the beginning phases of building your own business.

Chapter 2

Be Careful Who You Listen To

I want to share with you the number one reason people fail in their network marketing opportunity. It is likely not the company you have joined, or even the leader you have chosen to follow. It's not the product(s) or the service(s) they offer. More often than not, it is the people you let influence you, and those whose advice you decide to take. Please, be very careful when selecting the people you will listen to, especially if they have no idea what it is you are really trying to accomplish.

Parents, for example: Why would someone in their 30s join my business and then tell me that they require their mom or dad's permission?

Could your mother or father give you good advice on something they know nothing about? If you were sick, would they be able to prescribe the right medication for you? The right dose? The right duration? Would they know what to do if that prescription wasn't working? Would they know what to do if you got better but then regressed, and things got worse? Unless your parents are medical doctors, the answer is no.

The same can be said of business and finance. Unless your parents are wealthy and have successfully run a business, why would you expect them to be able to teach you how to *become* wealthy and/or run a successful business? And why would *they* think they could? Obviously they couldn't. And yet, the first people whose opinion and feedback we accept, in regards to reaching our goals, dreams, and aspirations are family members and our closest friends.

Remarkable, isn't it? Here's a thought: if it truly is your heart's desire to be successful in business and/or become financially independent, would it not make more sense to learn from someone who is successful in business and/or is financially independent? I would bet that it *does* makes sense to you, on a logical level. The good news is, in whatever business opportunity you have become involved, whatever company you have joined, there are probably great examples of people who have *become* successful in business, and are achieving financially independence.

When I was starting up, in the first network marketing company I joined, one of my very best friends came out to the first business presentation I attended. I trusted him and his judgment. We worked together in both the music business and the service station business, and I felt that he would be the first person to join me on this journey.

At the end of this incredible business meeting, he pulled me aside and said, "If you join this company, we can no longer be friends."

I have not spoken to him since that night. I think friendship is defined by never-ending support and non-judgment. I'm not insensitive. It *was* a tough decision, but it wasn't my decision, it was his.

The next story that I would like to share with you is about a young woman whom I recruited a number of years ago. For the purpose of the story, I will refer to her as "Sally". When I recruited Sally, she had joined with her fiance, as they were both eager to join in order to supplement their household income. Recruiting Sally while she was planning a wedding was probably not the best time for her. I understood this and just followed up with her occasionally until the timing was right.

During Sally's first six months with us, she got married and, unfortunately, separated; things were very difficult for her. She was a schoolteacher at the time and, when her husband moved out, she became solely responsible for all household expenses and bills. On her single income, that would have been impossible. Within six months, with my support and training, she was able to replace her teacher's salary of $40,000 per year. She then went full-time, and started to grow an incredible business. It took great commitment and sacrifice, during a dark time in her life, to achieve what Sally did.

Success has a way of shedding light into the dark moments of our lives. Here is the irony: even though her business prevented Sally from losing her home, and gave her independence and self-worth in a very sad time in her life, her family felt the need to have an "intervention" for her. They said that the business was controlling her life. What I want *you* to understand is that, if they are not in it, they cannot see it. They just can't grasp what it is you are trying to accomplish, and inevitably, what it will mean for both you and them. Sally's family acted out of love and concern. Not to damage, but to help. What they didn't have was her sense of urgency, which drove her to do what was needed to ensure her own success.

As I have previously illustrated, they were trying to prescribe medicine for her but did not understand the side effects of what they were prescribing. Now, almost seven years later, Sally is married to her business partner—the love of her life. They run a business that pays them in excess of $500,000 per year. They live in a beautiful home, drive beautiful cars, and have had their first child together. The same people who thought it necessary to stage an "intervention" are now her greatest supporters, and also get to enjoy the benefits of her success. Imagine the outcome if she had accepted their ultimatum when they'd given it, and quit!

There is something you need to know: no one knows *you* better than you! If you feel that being part of a business, and building something for yourself, is right for you, then why would you let someone else try to prescribe something different? You deserve the opportunity to change your life. Don't let your well-intentioned friends and family members mislead you with incomplete information. I know that's difficult, and I have seen people struggle with it for years. If I am clear about anything, though, it is that *you* know what is best for *you*.

I have two brothers and a sister, and all four of us are very different. How could any one of them give me advice on my life choices? Could my parents? Always remember that when people are giving you advice, they are giving it to you based on the experiences that *they* have had to date, which are not your experiences. They will also give advice out of fear of the unknown.

Our parents want us to be happy, but they want us to achieve that by doing things they understand. While it may be detrimental to us in the long run, the advice they give us is generally given with the best of intentions and the purest of motives. However, the choice to accept or decline that advice is ours. It is our responsibility to determine our own best course of action, make the decision to follow through, and just ask that they believe in us.

Live by this next statement in your career and you cannot fail: *There is no wrong decision in a commitment.* What I mean by that is that, morally and ethically, you always set out to finish what you start. I will share this statement frequently throughout the book, because it is important that you understand, clearly, that it takes decision and commitment to achieve success. The most important criteria for success is commitment. Action is a result of commitment, as committing to a cause or purpose means following a line of conduct.

Being committed could also be described as practicing your beliefs consistently. I have often said that commitment is "persistence with a purpose!" Any decision you make that is in line with your overall commitment is a decision worth making and sticking to.

This leads us to everyone else—extended family, friends, associates, and the people you try to recruit. Some of them may tell you that it's too good to be true, or that it's one of those pyramid things, but remember: unless those people are living the life you dream of having, *don't listen to them.*

Within my own circle of "well-meaning" people, it was my decision to better my life, in the manner I thought best, and their goal to try to stop me.

Sixteen years later, that former friend I told you about is still exactly where I left him—always struggling, in a career he doesn't like, working for what never seems to be enough money—while I have achieved success, and the ability to do great things: like send my children to private schools and give them the opportunity to travel with me all over the world, to places like Italy, Egypt, Turkey, and Greece. I've also reached a place, financially, where I am able to give back to the community, with various causes and charities, actually getting to see, with my own eyes, the substantial difference I have been able to make in people's lives.

I don't know what could be worth more than that.

This chapter, with all its pitfalls and warnings, lessons and potential rewards, describes just a small slice of the journey you may have to complete in order to achieve financial freedom and success. Please know that it is in your darkest moments where your strength is found. We only grow when life challenges us. There is no growth in coasting, only in climbing; and within the business you have joined, you will find all the tools you need to climb the mountains in front of you.

Always remember: there is no wrong decision in a commitment.

Chapter Three

Who Am I, And Who Do I Need To Be?

Now that we have addressed what you have joined, (or are considering joining) and the most challenging obstacles, we need to take a closer look at you.

After having had the opportunity to recruit and work with thousands of people, there is one common denominator that I see contributing to someone's failure: a lack of willingness to change. When you sign up to join a network marketing business, you join as the person you are—who you have come to be, at this time in your life. The knowledge and abilities you have acquired, up to this point, can only pay you as well as you have been paid. Therefore, it would stand to reason that, to make more money, you need to improve your abilities, and possibly use a different system to achieve your goals.

For example, if the most money you have ever made is $40,000 a year, then it stands to reason that the leadership skills you have honed and/or accumulated up until now can only allow you to continue earning the same.

For years, I have said the following in meetings: "You can't come into this business as you were and expect to get any more than you have ever had."

I believe the key ingredients to success are being able to expand your vision, improve your self-worth, and grow your leadership skills. This is easily said, of course. Make no mistake, it takes time and energy to make these changes happen. Your company, your leaders, and taking the opportunity to learn from self-improvement specialists, will help you down the path to personal growth.

In my experience, someone who has been used to living on $30,000 annually and manages to make $5,000 in a given month, will manage to sabotage themselves the following month so that they average themselves back to their familiar $2,500 monthly income—unless they have managed to expand their self-worth and self-respect to the point where they "believe" they are now worth $5,000 per month. The same goes for $10,000 per month, or $20,000 per month. That takes a lot more than desire ... it takes an overwhelming belief that you are worth every dollar of that monthly earning.

I *know* I'm worth *every penny* of the $90,000 per month that my business paid me last year. And since I'm constantly striving to improve my self-worth and belief, I will be perfectly comfortable taking that to a million per month. Make the decision to grow yourself—your perception of yourself, your belief in your worth, and your self-respect—so that you too will react correctly when financial success finds you. It reminds me of a popular self-improvement phrase, one that has even been made into an off-Broadway play: "I love you! You're perfect! Now change!"

Truth be told, you are perfect. You are the perfect person for getting you to where you are today. However, to excel and succeed requires growth. So make the decision to improve daily.

Coming from the service station business, and making about $80,000 per year, it would have been insane for me to think that, just because I joined a new business, I could suddenly make more money. This is the crux of the matter. Signing an application to join a business does not automatically give you the leadership skills necessary to step into this role. When someone joins a network marketing opportunity and fails, it is invariably because they were not prepared to make the changes necessary to succeed. This is why so many people refer to network marketing businesses as scams, cults, and pyramids ... not at all because of the company itself or the products/services it offers, but rather due to the number of people who refuse to commit themselves to a self-improvement regimen that fosters growth and change, and who subsequently fail.

Very early on in my network marketing career, it became clear to me that treating people like employees just does not work.

I had to become someone who authentically and legitimately cared about the people I was recruiting. It was important to always assure them that I was in the business *with* them and that they weren't doing this for me, but for themselves and their families. It is easy to say such a thing, but since people are naturally great at telling the difference between someone who is genuine and someone who is not, you must truly *mean* what you say. Make the conscious decision to care about the needs and feelings of your teammates and let this reflect in your speech and actions.

Not knowing what kind of person you are, I feel I would be doing you an injustice if I did not give you a list of who you need to be to become a great leader. Here's the secret: the more of these qualities you possess, the more money you will make, the more people you will help, and the more lives you will change. If you are not naturally blessed with the qualities in the following list, you can still achieve success. You may simply need to invest a little more time and energy into acquiring these important characteristics.

NON-JUDGEMENT: Great leaders never hold their people in judgement. It is not for us to judge another person's life choices or actions. We can never be certain what causes them to do what they do or think what they think. It's the job of a leader to find the positive in people, rather than the negative, and to see beyond their short-comings, fostering the goodness within them. I know this isn't easy. We live in a society that judges everyone. It's unfortunate that people just can't be themselves and live their own lives the way they choose. I encourage you to work on this quality daily, as it is one of the toughest to achieve. Trust me; people will know if you really stand in a place of non-judgement or if you're faking it. Faking is failing. Be real, and you never have to worry about being perfect.

As you work on being non-judgemental, you will learn a lot about yourself. The ability to "think about what you are thinking about" is known as Meta-cognition. If you practice meta-cognition, you will constantly be asking yourself why you are thinking the way you are; why you are letting yourself feel a certain way; and why you have given the comment or action of another person the meaning you have assigned it. An astute leader will echo the thinking of Swiss psychiatrist Carl Jung, who said: "Everything that irritates us about others can lead to an understanding of ourselves." Another powerful quote regarding judgment came from Mother Teresa: "If you judge people, you have no time to love them."

<u>FORGIVENESS:</u> Forgiving is forgetting. Forgiving is not something you say, it is something you do. Great leaders forgive quickly, and forget immediately. It's hard to lead someone that you hold a grudge over; that you feel has hurt you or betrayed you. Forgive now and forgive often.

If you are the type of person who naturally finds it difficult to forgive, I'd like to give you an analogy. Not forgiving someone is handcuffing yourself to them. Let me explain. The opposite of forgiveness is resentment. Resentment binds you to another person by a strong emotional link. That link is stronger than titanium. The person who is the object of your resentment has you locked up in that emotion and often are not even aware that they have this control or power over you. Forgiveness, pure and simple, is the only way to get free of that emotional bond and dissolve the link.

The next time you find yourself holding a grudge or feeling resentment, picture yourself chained to that individual. Do your best to understand the control you have handed them. The good news is that the handcuffs, which you have put on voluntarily and which lock you to the person who is the focus of your resentment, have a key. That key is forgiveness. People often confuse it with weakness, but resentment is the easiest thing in the world. Forgiveness is hard.

Mahatma Gandhi once said: "The weak can never forgive. Forgiveness is the attribute of the strong."

Are you a strong leader? Would you like to become a strong leader? Forgive often and forgive freely.

<u>UNDERSTANDING:</u> I know it's often hard to understand another person's perspective. The true art of understanding is not trying to understand at all. Therein lies the contradiction. It's actually the ability to accept that a person's perspective *is reality* as they see it. Understanding this truth heightens your

ability to accept that person's outlook, while not judging them. It also makes it substantially easier to forgive. Therefore, understanding is one of the building blocks of non-judgement and forgiveness.

I believe that truly knowing another person is impossible when based solely on what they say and reveal about themselves. Instead, it comes from knowing the things they *cannot* reveal about themselves. To understand them, you can't just listen to what a person says, especially since most people hear only what they can understand. The challenge is to look at anything we do *not* understand, and *then* really listen.

Marie Curie described it well: "Nothing in life is to be feared. It is only to be understood."

Be a fearless leader while endeavoring to understand your people, and what they aspire to be.

ACCEPTANCE: People will be and do as they choose. No one will ever do anything according to your agenda; they are too busy worrying about their own. People will only do what makes sense to them. Accept that. It's easier to accept people's choices than it is to try and change them. I learned a long time ago that if *you* say something, people might doubt it. When *they* say it, it's true. Accept people for all they are, all they do, and all they are going to do.

How can you accept a person who is very different from you, or even the completely opposite, in what they do, say, and think? The truth of the matter is that accepting any other human being into your life is a conscious decision, knowing that inevitable differences in taste and opinion will exist, and may need to *coexist*.

George Orwell said that the ability to "hold two contradictory beliefs in one's mind simultaneously, and accept both of them" is one of the qualities of a good leader.

Being a good leader will, undoubtedly, involve knowing that your people do things for their own reasons and according to their own agendas, and accepting that fact.

EMPATHY: Empathy, in this context, is the ability to lead with care and concern, without being enrolled in another persons' problem or challenge. We live in a world where people long to have their feelings validated. Learn to listen, and hear with understanding and non-judgement; hear with forgiveness and acceptance of the individual's feelings and the challenges they are experiencing. This is true caring leadership.

Why empathy and not sympathy? While they are both acts of feeling, they are very different. Sympathy means feeling *for* the person; you're sorry *for* them or pity them. However, you may not understand what they're feeling, or why. Since we often can't understand what a person is dealing with, we may have little choice but to sympathize. However, it takes real work, and imagination (or having lived through a similar experience) to be able to truly empathize.

Empathy is best described as feeling *with* the person ... a big difference from feeling for a person. With empathy, you have a good sense of what they feel, know why they feel it, and perhaps even understand their feelings to a degree.

The major difference is that, with sympathy, since you feel *for* the person, their current situation will impact, and possibly temper, your communication with them.

Someone with sympathy may say, "I am so sorry for you." This leaves the person feeling alone or isolated in their grief.

(To be purely practical for a moment, in terms of a business difficulty this can create, if you have a product or service that might benefit an individual for whom you have sympathy, you will likely shy away from offering it, since you feel bad for the person.)

An empathic person will be able to connect honestly, and say, "I've had the exact same thoughts" or "I totally get what you're saying" or "I know how you feel, because I've felt that too." This reassures the individual that they are not alone, and that others truly get how they're feeling. It also allows you not to lose yourself in their grief, so that you may still deliver your message.

Make no mistake. Empathy is a key to understanding others, accepting them, and forgiving them. It is a hallmark of a great leader.

DISCIPLINE: The ultimate divider of success and failure is discipline. Self-discipline, as it relates to the above list, will be one of your biggest challenges. The ability to master

non-judgement, forgiveness, acceptance, and empathy will be what will set you apart from all other leaders. Discipline is the fine art of self-management: being empathetic when we want to be sympathetic; accepting when we don't want to accept; forgiving people we feel are unworthy of forgiveness; not judging when judgement seems to be the only option; and caring just for the pure sense of caring. This is outward discipline.

Inward discipline is your ability to do what you said you were going to do, and to do it in spite of challenges or obstacles. There always seems to be good reasons to *not* fulfill your commitments and hold to the disciplines that surround them. You must have a *better* reason to keep your word, to continue your self-discipline, and live up to your full potential. Great leaders have mastered the art of keeping their word.

That was a brief outline of the characteristics you need to possess in order to be successful in your network marketing business. Notice that I did not say you need to become an incredible salesperson and public speaker, or someone who is outwardly charismatic. If I could build the perfect recruit, they would, instead, possess the original qualities I listed—from non-judgemental to disciplined. The world needs more people that live these qualities.

As you start incorporating these traits,your business will become one that is built on the "law of attraction." People will be attracted to your sincere nature. They will want to be around you to support you in your business. This will create a true sense of following. As a result, once you master this list, your skills in regards to selling and public speaking, or lack thereof, will become irrelevant.

The ultimate objective is to have people do what you want them to do, and have them think they wanted to do it. This is not a negative statement, and it is not manipulation. I became successful by wanting to help my leaders from the music industry, the service station industry, and the network marketing industry. It is a contagious feeling—wanting to help people succeed. Very quickly, my key people grabbed that feeling and ran with it, doing all they could to help me succeed, with the understanding that they would inevitably succeed as well, as a by-product of their activity.

It will take time and practice to perfect, but the rewards that await you will make the journey worthwhile.

Where to start? List the above qualities on a piece of paper, and affirm to yourself that this is the person you are. Remind yourself daily, even hourly, that you are the leader you wish to become. Convince yourself that you have discipline and empathy, that you accept people as they are, that you are ready to forgive and do not judge. Put reminder notes everywhere, listing these traits. Make it the background on your computer, laptop, and phone. Persuade your personality that these qualities, and any others of importance to you, are yours *today*. Not tomorrow. Today! You *will* start hearing different, more positive, comments.

"You've changed."

"You seem happier."

"It's so nice to be around you."

When you meet new people, they will say things like: "I feel like I have known you forever."

Who you are right now is not nearly as important as who you are going to be. For years, I have heard this said (within network marketing companies): "You are one recruit away from an explosion." The disclaimer they all seem to leave out is this:

You *are* the one recruit away from the explosion!

When you become your best recruit, many will join you. You have no right to recruit a phenomenal person into *your* business until you have become a phenomenal person in someone *else's*. Become that great person to your recruiter, and allow the "law of attraction" to motivate other great individuals to join you.

Chapter Four

Belief

Belief, to me, is the number one reason why the world is the way it is. People stopped believing long ago. If you truly want to be successful and change your life, you need to have an unshakable belief in the company you are joining. Unfortunately, this generally means that, initially, you must have *blind* faith, which some people may be uncomfortable with. Don't be afraid to stand up for something. Our world has become a middle class society of followers. Find your way out of the crowd by standing up for something. If you have selected a network marketing opportunity as your vehicle out of mediocrity, then wholeheartedly get behind it and support it.

I truly believe that people today are lost. Their circumstances, situations, and finances have made their career choices for them. If you could go back, would you have chosen something different for your career? The better part of the population would answer affirmatively. That is why belief becomes so important when starting your own business. Success is a psychological journey. It's not a destination. It's not a certain amount of money, a car, a home, a boat, or a trophy spouse. It's a journey of belief and the conquering of all obstacles put before you.

I would like to share a story of belief with you. A number of years ago, I took my oldest daughter, Eponine, on a trip to Egypt. Please note that the information I learned during my visit, which I am now sharing with you, may not actually be historical fact, but the message had a profound impact on my life either way. We toured the better part of Egypt—Cairo, Luxor, the Valley of the Kings—and cruised down the Nile. Living in North America, we are greatly sheltered from true poverty, and this was my first experience seeing it.

As we toured the temples and tombs, I was in awe of the incredible history and workmanship, as well as the preservation of that workmanship. I also found myself noticing all the intricate detail, from the perfectly matched stone columns to the beautiful artwork on the walls.

As we progressed in the tour, and moved on to next temple, I noticed that the columns, although still in perfect form, no longer matched. It was as if this temple had been built with a mismatched set of columns. I asked our tour guide, who was an Egyptologist, why this temple's columns were different and didn't match, when all the previous temples' had matched perfectly.

"It's simple," he replied. "The Egyptian people built the temples in worship of their gods. At some point, before the fall of the Egyptian empire, they had built an alliance with Greece, and the Egyptian people were forced to build temples not just for Egyptian gods, but for Greek gods as well. This was not in alignment with their belief systems, so the workmanship became shoddier—less precise."

I understood this immediately, and how it could be applied to North American society. People don't do things because they believe in them anymore; they do them for money.

Although many people in society deny that they work for money, because it just doesn't sound right, it's only semantics—a play on words inside their minds. If you are working to pay your mortgage, buy groceries, make car payments, pay utilities, and cover all other essentials of life, then the bad news is: you work for money.

If you did not need money, would you still go to work tomorrow? Or would you seek out something that you love to do to fill your time?

This is where your choice to start your own home-based, or network marketing business, and your willingness to believe wholeheartedly in that choice, can fundamentally give you your life back. Like the Egyptians, we are forced to build for false gods ... mortgage, cars, bills, and so on. Happiness is found in the process of growth, self-improvement, and change. Happiness is not found trapped in the closet, or prison cell, called mediocrity. Finding your life's purpose will allow you to obtain true wealth.

How do you wholeheartedly commit and believe? You just do! You may also refer to it as faith. Faith can be defined as: "a confident belief in the truth, value, or trustworthiness of a person, idea, or thing. Belief does not rest on logical proof or material evidence."

In regards to your new business opportunity, that is how you *must* feel. Right now it is just a vision, an opportunity. However, you have to have absolute belief that this can be your reality, and be willing to support that belief with action and a strong work ethic. The stronger your belief, the more powerful your faith will be.

To illustrate: although I have never seen, nor spoken, to God, I wholeheartedly believe in Him. I believe; therefore I have faith. When I started, 16 years ago, the two most important sentences I heard were the following: "There is nothing more powerful than a made-up mind" and "You must have an unfaltering belief in the company and the products".

Making up your mind and having an unfaltering belief are conscious decisions. I challenge you, right now, to make up your mind regarding your business opportunity; decide that it is the vehicle you will use to achieve your goals and dreams, and stick with it regardless of challenges and obstacles. Believe in it, and never lose that belief. Commit to yourself that you will allow nothing to impact that belief.

In closing this chapter, I want to leave you with a simple insight. I am not naive enough to believe everything everyone has ever said to me. I'm also not fool enough to *not* check the truth or accuracy of what people tell me for myself.

Here's the secret: believe everything you are told until you have unquestionably proven it to be false. This means falling into action, not into research. Just because it is on the Internet does not mean that it is true. Be a person who makes decisions based on indisputable, profound knowledge, not hearsay, innuendo, or gossip.

Be steadfast. Don't let others steal your future.

Learn by doing, not by assuming.

Choose to believe until you have a sound reason not to. There is no wrong decision in a commitment, and you will likely never find a reason to not believe.

Chapter Five

Getting Off To A Fast Start

So far, we have discussed the initial challenges you may face, the obstacles you may need to overcome, and the importance of people skills, people management, and belief. It is now time to truly get started.

This is the meat and potatoes of building a network-marketing business.

It's time to create a list: of everyone you know—family, friends, neighbors, old school-chums, co-workers at your current place of employment, and so on.

I'm sure that as soon as you read that last sentence, you will be asking: "What do you mean create a list? You already told me that my friends and family would likely challenge my decision to start my own business!"

Although that's true, it is still the best way to get started. It's your relationship equity that you need to capitalize on initially. This is not a bad thing. If you truly believe in the company, their products, and their services, this should not be difficult for you.

The good news is that this is like ripping off a bandage. It hurts less if you do it quick.

When I transitioned full-time into network marketing, I had just gone through some of the worst financial times in my life. My credibility was definitely not at its highest. Still, I was determined to follow the guidance of my leader and put together the best list possible. I certainly learned a lot about my family and friends through that initial list!

Let's be honest, our friends and family will be the first to gossip about us.

Here's a little secret: if somebody is willing to gossip to you, they are probably willing to gossip about you. One of the most important things you will need to remember is that your reputation isn't yours; it is made up of other people's opinions of your actions and choices. They will create their opinions based on judgement, without understanding what would ever cause you to feel, think, or do the things you do. Don't feel bad; everyone is talking about somebody at some point. It's just unfortunate that they are doing it without an understanding of what the underlying conditions really are.

Now, why would I get into all of that when I am just asking you to make a list? It's simple. People do not like to make a list for one reason, and one reason only:

They are afraid of what people will think of them.

Yes, this is true of you too. Unfortunately, we are all concerned with our stature in the eyes of our friends and family. This does not mitigate or minimize the importance of creating a great list. My advice: give everyone in your life the chance to say no. If you truly believe in the company and the products, this should not be an issue.

For example, if you had a cure for cancer, would you not tell everybody? Of course you would. And who would you call first? Unquestionably, your family and closest friends. So, if you are willing to put forth the effort to build a great business, make the decision to start with those same people. Remember, there is no wrong decision in a commitment, so commit to this and win.

Don't be afraid of a little rejection. In the end, it will become completely meaningless. When I first went full-time with my network marketing business, I truly learned about character. For example, I remember calling one of my dearest friends, and asking her to let me come over and do a business presentation, for a new business venture I was very excited about. She actually laughed when I requested her help.

I believe that no matter what I did, this person would have reacted the way she did, due to her inability to make her own sound choices. I don't see it as her laughing at me. I see it as her laughing at herself, because of her own insecurities and potential inability to say no if I actually did a presentation for her. Her only recourse to compensate for that insecurity was to insult me, and avoid the issue completely.

The next example was my ex-wife's best friend. This person truly owed me a favor. When she was in college, she was taking an advertising course and there were a few occasions when she had called upon me for favors. She had asked me to buy advertising space from her as part of her training experience. On every occasion, I did so quite willingly. In my mind, she was certainly someone who would be willing to help me with my training, as I helped her with hers. Unfortunately, she never even returned my phone calls. When I did manage to reach her, she deflected by saying she needed to talk to her husband, who happened to be my cousin. She didn't even have the decency to call me back to say she wasn't interested. I share this with you so that you clearly understand that, no matter what you do or say, you will never know who is willing to support you, and who is not.

The lesson is: don't pre-judge. You never know who may or may not be willing to look at doing something different. Here's another good example. I was not actually even recruited into the business that I joined. I replied to a newspaper ad. Think about this for a minute: up to that point, I had spent 9 years in the retail service station business and was only prospected once by the company I ended up joining. It was the worst attempt at prospecting ever. A regular customer pulled into my service station, handed me a magazine, and said:

"My wife has joined this new exciting business. I will have her call you."

I took the magazine, gave him my business card, and didn't hear another word, or even look at the magazine, until three years later.

I joined the company and saw the same magazine sitting in our office. Something I found even more interesting is that a guy I grew up with had joined the same company at around the same time as I started my service station business. He spent almost two years trying to recruit my brother, who had just graduated from university, but did not attempt to contact me to share the opportunity.

He had pre-judged me. He thought I wasn't the right type of person for his business. The ironic part is that I bumped into him a few years ago at a large conference I was hosting. At this point, I was making around a million dollars a year. He told me the story that I have just shared with you. I think my point is clear ... give everyone the chance to say no. Don't do what my friend did and pre-judge. If he had recruited me, he would be financially independent today just from compensation from my business.

This is the reason why everyone you know *must* go on your list. The examples I shared are two of many I could have used. The ironic part is that most of the people I put on my list, who I was certain would help me in my new venture, did not support me or get involved. The people I decided to put on my list just to fill in the blanks ending up becoming the people I built a business with.

ASK EVERYBODY

I think you should be getting the picture now. Some will support you, and some won't. Do it anyway.

Let's break down some key components to developing your market:

1. Make a list of everyone who would know your name.

I teach my people to write down absolutely everyone they know by name, and who would recognize them and/or their name. Yes, even just first names. With this method, most people I recruited were able to create a list of 30 to 50 names, and many were able to reach 100 or more. If you are married, can you find your list of wedding invitees? That should be a great place to start. You bought them dinner and entertained them for an evening, so they may be open to the concept of at least looking at the opportunity that has you so fired up.

Here's how I would expand the list further: find and use some manner of memory jogger to spawn creativity in the creation of the list. Or, think of the people that your spouse, parents, children, or siblings know. Could you, hypothetically, call the friend of your sister and say:

"Hi Carol. Ray Young here. I'm Greg's younger brother. Listen, I only have a minute, but I'm looking to expand my business and I was curious if you were looking to … (proceed with your company's standard presentation)."

2. <u>Do not decide what others would be willing to do or not willing to do. Give them the opportunity to say no.</u>

Frankly, if you made the decision to not call me because you thought you already knew what my response would be, I cannot tell you how annoyed that would make me. Personally, I do not think you have the right to make a decision for me. Give me the information, and I will make a decision, right or wrong, that suits me. You owe it to your family, friends, and acquaintances to do your due diligence in presenting them with your opportunity, and allow them to decide.

3. <u>Always be on the lookout to expand your list: from your auto-mechanic to your grocery clerk; your dentist to your doctor; to your kids' friends' parents, etc..</u>

I have had teammates who would dedicate an hour or two per day to prospect and add new names to their list. I have also had those who did not set aside specific times to prospect, but had the mentality of always being on the lookout for people to talk to. They had their radar going constantly. Either way, you run across people every day who could be engaged in conversation, and with a couple of key leading questions, could be introduced to your opportunity.

4. <u>Be creative.</u>

Here's what I have learned about recruiting. Everything works sometimes. From newspaper ads, to trade shows, to friends and family, to starting up a conversation while at your son or daughter's soccer game. And always be professional.

Let me share a great example of prospecting and networking. When I first joined the network marketing industry, I wanted to expand my market through my friends and family. However,

I learned quickly that friends and families do not like to share names and numbers of their extended relationships. Being naturally shy, I could not see myself cold prospecting (going out and introducing myself to random people), so I had to get creative. Therefore, I took every opportunity to attend social events where I could possibly meet new people.

For example, a friend had invited me to a barbecue for someone's birthday. I attended it with a purpose of networking without directly prospecting. There was a guy named Cliff who was doing the barbecuing. I started a conversation with him—general small talk. We then got on the topic of cars.

At the time I was driving an Audi TT Roadster convertible, by which he was highly impressed. I then asked him, "What is your dream car?" He told me it would be a brand new Corvette convertible. The conversation continued for about 15 or 20 minutes, all about cars.

Then I asked him, "What are you currently doing for a living?"

"I'm a tool and die maker," he replied.

"That sounds like a pretty good job," I continued. "Will it ever pay you enough to buy that Corvette?"

Our conversation continued, and the event went on and inevitably ended. Note: I did not prospect him or ask him for his number at the barbecue.

The next day, I called my friend to thank her for the prior evening. I then proceeded to ask her for Cliff's number. I told her that Cliff and I were talking about cars and that I wanted to follow up on our conversation. She willingly gave me his number.

Due to my approach, there was no concern that I was trying to prospect him for my network marketing business. I proceeded to call Cliff, reintroducing myself on the phone, and asked him plainly: "If I could show you a way to get your Corvette, would you give me half an hour to give you the details?"

After the meeting, Cliff joined my business and became an integral part of growing my network marketing company.

5. Have a sense of urgency with moral and ethics.

Don't make people feel uncomfortable. Treat them the way you would like to be treated.

I share this next story with you to illustrate a bad marketing experience I witnessed. A few months before I joined my network marketing company, I was at a christening for my wife's second cousin. It was a beautiful sunny day and we sat in the backyard, with family and friends, celebrating this special moment. Unfortunately, it became clouded by the actions of this precious little girl's grandfather who had recently started selling life insurance. He thought it was appropriate to do the rounds of the guests handing out business cards and explaining why they needed to call him about life insurance.

I was not aware at the time, but he taught me a valuable lesson that saved me from making a million mistakes, and helped me to make millions of dollars. Be creative but don't be offensive. No one wants to feel like you're only talking to him or her in order to close a sale, or to get him or her to join a business they are not familiar with. There is a proper time and place for everything.

6. Social media, Facebook, text messaging, twitter, and emails are a great way of opening up the lines of communication, especially with those you have not connected with in a while. Do not, however, hide behind these forms of communication.

In the end, the fastest way to success is the old fashioned way. Pop by, visit a friend, make a phone call, or invite somebody for coffee. I know this may feel uncomfortable. Trust me; I have not forgotten what it was like when I made my first list.

I put people on it that I had not spoken to in years, from family members whom I thought would think I was crazy, to people who I thought would laugh at me. More often than not, I got it wrong.

I would sit in my study on Sunday nights to line up my week. I would make phone calls until I finally got a positive response. Sometimes the only positive response I would hear would be something as simple as: "Give me a call next week and I will let you know."

I know that that's still not a yes, but it's way closer to it than "No way man, forget it."

Another piece of advice: Keep your list on paper. Our society is "tech-savvy" today, and our inclination may be to keep our list in our laptop or smart-phone. I recommend against this. Always having a list on paper does a few things.

First, the list in your pocket or purse will be a constant reminder to focus on prospecting. Every time you see it, you will be put back into prospecting mode. Since we are so accustomed to having our Blackberries and iPhones with us, this effect is missing.

Secondly, the names on the list will begin to haunt you (for lack of a better word). You will begin to get sick and tired of seeing the same names on the list, if they are there after a week or two. You will want to make the call just to get the name off the list. It will get to the point that you will make the call and say:

"Mike, I put your name on my list of people to call to show my business to, and frankly, whether you're interested or not is immaterial ... I just want 20 minutes over coffee to run it by you so I can scratch your name off my list!"

I can't tell you how many appointments I've set up with that approach, all because I just couldn't stand to see their name on my list anymore.

Here's the secret: never finish your call session on a negative call. Make as many calls as is necessary to end on a positive note. Let me give you another example to illustrate.

My daughters take horseback-riding lessons. At about eight years of age, my daughter Kassidy was thrown off of a horse, and did a face plant into the dirt. She got up crying, with dirt stuck in her helmet and in her face, and was clearly very distraught. As her father, I wanted to jump into the arena and run to her rescue, but her very skilled and professional coach made sure that the only focus was to get her back on the horse. Kassidy's coach knew, without question, that if she left the arena without getting back on the horse, she might never ride again. Today, thanks to her coach's push to end that lesson on a positive note, Kassidy still loves horseback riding.

Recently we were in the Turks and Caicos Islands, and Kassidy rode a horse bareback along the ocean shore—an experience she would have missed out on if not for her strong discipline and commitment, and the insight of her coach. What experiences will you miss out on, if you don't acknowledge the fear and do it anyway? Pick up the phone; make the calls, develop contacts on your list, or eliminate them from your list due to lack of interest. Either way, get on with it. Don't miss out on the greatest experience of your life by worrying what someone might think of you. It's your ability to have and maintain a sense of urgency that will help you succeed.

You will always be your best at the start of something new. Look at any relationship you have ever been in. Early on, you are your best you. Therefore, the time is now. Be your best. Do your best with urgency and clarity, and the future is yours.

Chapter Six

Relationships

We all have different personalities. Some people are very action orientated, some want to focus on structure and stability, some are technically minded, and others are relationship orientated. It truly doesn't matter what type of person you recruit, as it relates to this chapter about building relationships.

The bottom line is: people don't quit on friends. This is where it becomes paramount not just to recruit people, but to truly build and have an authentic relationship with them. To achieve this, the first thing you must understand is that everyone is different. I know you know this on a basic level. However, when it comes to building your business, understanding the different types of personalities, and how to communicate which each type, is of crucial importance. Some are going to want to talk about changing the world and doing great things together. Technical and analytical people will want to know specific information about why, and how, everything works the way it does. Structured people are always conscious of the security of their families, and will want to know that their family will be more stable by their being part of your business . Finally, there are the action-based people who don't care what you are going to say or do, but will just go and do it anyway.

Do you know which type you are? Now, think about your work colleagues, closest friends, your immediate and extended family members. Could you say with any certainty which type of personality they have? Now, think about your business, and consider how you might "tweak" your presentation to suit each of the four described personality types. For example, if your prospect exhibits the type of personality characteristics that suggest that the financial security of the family is of paramount importance, will you discuss changing the world? Or how the web-site works? Or how they get to run their own show, be the captain of their own ship, and build a huge, massive, thriving business? I wouldn't. I would explain that by getting involved with me, they have an opportunity to solidify their family's financial future.

The following list of relationship-building questions may not be suitable for all network marketing companies. It is still in alignment with prospecting and getting to know people. I will explain my thoughts on the best way to recruit someone into a network marketing opportunity. Please feel free to take the parts that suit your business and company.

An analogy first: if you went to see a really great movie and you wanted to get your best friend to go, would you tell them everything about it, up to and including the ending? If you would, then you suck as a friend. Now your friend is going to waste $15, because you told them too much. I'm kidding, but don't miss the point. The best way to accomplish your goal is to tease them with just enough information to capture their interest and curiosity, and no more.

If it is going to take three hours to explain everything about your business to a new recruit, friend, or family member, you need to do it over several meetings. Allow me to explain. I believe the first meeting regarding your business opportunity should be very little about the opportunity, and a whole lot about your new recruit. I know that sounds strange ... how do I recruit a person if I don't talk about my company and products? Simple. Ask them questions. You can identify what type of personality they are, what their "hot buttons" are, and how to best support them.

Over the years, I have watched associates "throw up" on others about their business opportunity. If I taught it once, I have taught it a million times. DON'T THROW UP ON PEOPLE! Give them just enough to capture their interest and curiosity.

Let me give you a list of some of the questions that could be asked *prior* to asking someone to join your business:

1. How long have you been in your career?

2. What do you love most about your career? What do you like least about your career?

3. If money were not an issue, what would be the first thing you would do or buy?

4. Do you see yourself staying in the position you are in for the rest of your life? If not, what are your plans to change it?

5. What are your favorite things to do in your spare time?

6. Is spending more time with your family important?

7. What did you dream your life would be like when you were younger? How close is it to that vision?

8. Describe your dream home.

9. Is paying for your children's education important to you?

10. What is your perfect automobile?

11. Is leaving a legacy for your children and/or grandchildren important to you?

12. How about important causes, churches, or charities?

13. Where on the planet have you always wanted to visit, but haven't yet had the opportunity?

14. Do you have any favorite hobbies, like flying, scuba-diving, cruising, or water-skiing?

This is just a small list, but I think you are getting the point. Be very clear about the importance of who you are and why you are doing what you are doing. Don't be afraid to be authentic because people can tell if you are not. Get to know your new recruit, even if it's a close family member or a friend, because you wouldn't know the answer to a lot of those questions without asking. Don't assume you know the answers.

By the time you complete this first meeting, your goal is to have enticed them to see you again. I refer to this as "closing to the next meeting". That meeting could be another one-on-one appointment, where you further elaborate on the business plan, or a more formal business overview, where you present products and services. In the second meeting, as long as you're sincere about wanting to help them achieve their goals, your potential recruit will feel as if they have known you for a long time, and that you have a great business connection. Sincerity leads to success.

I had a person in my business who made $50,000 in his first year, which is not an unreasonable amount of money to earn in your first year in network marketing. The funny thing was that he and his wife were prospecting and recruiting 15-20 times more people than other people in my business who were making $200,000 a year. It was easy to figure out that he didn't care about people and that he was faking it. I believe he is on his fourth or fifth business opportunity since leaving my business. Here's another little secret for you. It's likely not the wrong opportunity; it's likely the wrong person.

So far, we have had a meeting to get to know our new person, learn some details about them, determine their personality type, and pique their interest enough to meet with us again. The second meeting may be when we discuss the business in detail, the products and/or services the company offers, and the likely compensation available. We will now be able to do this particularly well, since we know their personality, and the issues and concerns that are most important to *them*—rather than to *us*. If the reason that *we* are in the business is to be our own boss, run the show, and make a lot of money, but the prospect sitting across from us has a different agenda, you do yourself and your opportunity a disservice by bringing them up. Focus on what your business will do for *them!*

If your prospect is eager to start, you may now sign them up. Personally, I would "close to the next meeting" once again.

This now leads to the third meeting: the "game plan". This is when you will help your new recruit create their warm market list and establish a plan to help them achieve their goals and dreams.

As I said previously, you can do this all in one meeting, but if your approach is too aggressive it could lead to something we refer to as "buyer's remorse."

For example, I watched one of my associates bring in a person who was answering a "Help Wanted" ad she had posted. As stated, I train my people diligently on the importance of the first meeting being a series of questions about your prospect, and little else. For seven years, this particular associate of mine had witnessed me doing this. The prospect arrived and was in the interview with the associate for more than two hours. The prospect, a well-dressed young gentlemen who was eagerly looking for an opportunity, later emerged—scurrying out of the office to the back parking lot.

Already knowing the answer, I asked my associate how it had gone.

"Amazing," she said. "He's in, and he is so excited."

"Why were you in there so long?" I asked.

"He just wanted to know everything and get started."

"Great, what's next?"

"He's just gone out to his car to get his phone, so that he can make his warm market list with me."

"Wow," I said. "Warm market list already, on the first appointment! That doesn't usually work."

In her very smug English-accented tone she said, "I guess you are always right about everything, aren't you?"

"I guess I'm not," I replied. The words had barely fallen from my lips before we watched him speed out of the parking lot, with tires squealing, never to be seen again.

All he had been waiting for was an opportunity to leave the office. My associate had basically been holding him prisoner. DON'T DO THIS! This associate inevitably failed and left the business, all because of her lack of willingness to build relationships with people before asking for a cheque.

If you are serious about building a business, always take the time necessary to build a strong foundation, to build a relationship. Remember, friends don't quit on friends. By taking what could be done in one single three-hour meeting and spreading it out over a number of face-to-face meetings, you create a true relationship with that individual. The commodity that network marketing companies trade is not their product and services, it is the people who choose to wholeheartedly join and build a business within their organization. Therefore, that is also *your* commodity.

Building relationships extends beyond a person's introduction to your business, and includes those who are now within your business. Social functions are paramount in strengthening the unity of your organization. When I first started, I had very little money, which meant that taking people out to dinner, lunches, and coffee was not financially feasible. Instead, we opted to hold pot-luck get-togethers, euchre tournaments, and barbecues. As a group, my key leaders and I would meet at our office every morning at seven, to walk together while listening to motivational and inspirational CDs. This created a bond between us, as we shared insights regarding what we had listened to that day. This also created a sense of unity.

Unity eliminates insecurity. People want to feel a part of something. So make them feel included and inclusive. It's important that you maintain daily contact with your active associates. Then maintain weekly contact with those less active, and monthly contact with the fence-sitters. Follow-up is imperative. People will move at their own pace, not yours.

I had a person in my business named Rod. I'd met him through a mutual friend, and followed all the criteria for building a relationship. The timing just wasn't right for him. In the two years it took me to recruit him into my business, I watched him go from starting a new business, which he was very excited about, to shutting down that same business. He ended up depressed, working in a temporary agency for $10 an hour, and hating his life. Then he got a reasonably good job, working in a factory for $70,000 a year. Unfortunately, it immediately reminded him why he had started his own business in the first place—he did not enjoy factory work.

Over that two-year period, we met once a month for a coffee and, in most meetings, I did not mention my business opportunity to him. I talked to him constantly about where he was at in his life. After he finally joined my business, in 2004, he became one of the biggest leaders and recruiters in our company. He surpassed $250,000 a year in income. Compensation from his business was paying me close to $200,000 per year. Let's do the math on the 25 coffees I invested in this now long-time friend. $200,000 per year is roughly $16,700 per month, and divided by 25 coffees that comes to about $667 per coffee. That's $667 for each and every coffee I bought Rod during that two-year period, paid to me every month since 2004. Some of you might call an individual two or three times, get some indifference or indecision, call the person a flake, and just forget about them. Have I demonstrated what a mistake that could be?

Your goal is to help people move beyond the fears and limitations that could be stopping them from joining you in business. Your job as a leader is to get people to stick around long enough to realize they are good enough to do this, and begin to experience success. Never underestimate the power of desire. It supersedes skill, knowledge, and fear. It is the driving factor for change.

"The future does not belong to the faint hearted. It belongs to the brave."

~ Ronald Reagan

Chapter Seven

Building A Legacy

Every network marketing company, and its leaders, will have a system for you to follow. That is why I have avoided sharing systems in this book. My goal was to give you the information that many systems overlook. The best systems will not teach you interpersonal skills, how to overcome concerns and issues, to deal with rejection, or how to grow into a strong leader. The people you recruit into your business will invariably require and value a sound leader. Many people will join a network marketing company and come in with great enthusiasm. Their 'want' is unquestionable, but wanting something isn't good enough. The greatest of intentions are overshadowed by the least of actions. The people who act continually, consistently, and consciously will win. Doing the same thing over and over again, even when that action seems repetitive and tedious, will help you build a legacy.

The gift of network marketing is creating multiple streams of income, from multiple potential outlets. It may offer an infrastructure that will allow you to build a business internationally without leaving your home. It will give you the ability to have recognition, and to have your family and friends be proud of you, but more importantly, for you to be proud of yourself—to know that you overcame the obstacles, challenges, naysayers, and people who tried to stop you in your quest for freedom.

A legacy is something more than just money and it's more than just a business. It's knowing that you took what you knew to be your life and turned it into something extraordinary; it's becoming an example of willingness and determination, of goal setting and goal reaching, of commitment and follow-through. This business, in which you may have set out to make some part-time money, could very well transform into something full-time. To do otherwise would be like leaving a Ferrari in the garage and never starting it. The business vehicle you are in will create financial freedom for anyone. You just need to take it out of the garage and hit the highway. Your business does not discriminate on the basis of race, sex, or education. It gives all an equal opportunity.

The *only* way it differentiates is in terms of work ethic. Put your work ethic into fifth gear and watch what your business vehicle will do for you!

Do you have what it takes to juggle your full-time job, your family responsibilities, your finances, and your new voluntary career? Only you can answer that truthfully. Here are some basic *daily* activities that can simplify the process of building a legacy that goes beyond just a paycheque.

1. Become a student. Read for at least 20 minutes a day—books on leadership, and information as it relates to your chosen company.

2. Make a list, every night before you go to bed, of the 10 most important people (relating to your business) with whom you need to communicate the next day. The importance of doing it the night before is that you will feel more open to listing uncomfortable calls. Be committed

to this daily routine.

3. Edify your upline. Always speak highly of *your* leader, even when you are uncertain of his or her motives. The moment you speak negatively of your leader, your people will never be able to listen to them again. Great leaders were once great followers. Follow well so that you can lead well.

4. Boring makes you money. Follow up—over and over again.

5. On the last day of every month, create a list of all your potential sales and/or recruits—which I refer to as a possibility log. This also needs to be completed before you go to bed on the last day of every month.

I live by the above list of activities. When I first started my network marketing career, I worked part-time. I was actually a full-time stay-at-home dad. I was going through a terrible time financially and, because I was in a career change, my wife had to go back to her job prior to the end of her maternity leave. These were tough times for my family and me, yet I exercised sufficient discipline to adhere to the above list, ensuring change to my family's financial future. You can do this. I completed all the things that I needed to in 10 hours per week and built a business worth millions of dollars. It paid me as high as a million dollars in a single year.

Building a legacy means becoming a master of people-development skills. All the information in this book is designed to give you those tools and, in addition to your company's system and your leader's support, your success is inevitable.

To build a legacy you don't need to be the prettiest, the tallest, the smartest, the best public speaker, or the best salesperson. You simply need to be the most committed. Remember that there is no wrong decision in a commitment. Although I have repeated this statement over and over again, people just don't get it. To decide is simple. I have found that people can get their mouths to say anything. Saying "yes" is easy. However, without commitment, your ability to stick to your decision when times get tough will be nonexistent.

Build a business, be proud of all that you are, and accept all that you are not. Then begin reading with the goal of improving your leadership skills, and make small but perceptible improvements in your abilities as a great recruit. Dazzle your upline with your conscientiousness, attention to detail, punctuality, and commitment to completing your tasks. Appreciate every pothole in the road, every mountain you need to climb, and every relationship you get the chance to mold.

Chapter Eight

Be The Dream

This chapter may not be the most important, from the perspective of building your business and becoming a great leader, but—emotionally—it's everything.

We all have dreams. Unfortunately, every year we are one year closer to the end of our lives. We see it getting less and less likely that we will ever get to live our dreams. That is when people start to give up. I urge you, whether you are 20 years old or 50 years old, or any age in between or beyond that, take your dreams back!

Here is what I have learned. When I first got into business for myself, I realized that my dreams could come back. I had the ability to dream again. Unfortunately, in the world we live in, most of our dreams come with a price tag. When you are stuck in a job with bills and responsibilities that never let you see beyond those realities, it's hard to fantasize beyond them as well.

I started to dream immediately about making enough money that my wife could stay at home and raise our children, instead of a $10-an-hour daycare provider. I dreamed of travel; I dreamed of a nice home and a nice car; I dreamed of making a difference in our community and with charities that meant something to me. Also, I dreamed of sending my children to private schools.

Let's see how it worked out.

My ex-wife left the job that she hated. My situation had forced her to go back to work, so that I could build the business that inevitably freed her from a career and a commute she did not like. Today she runs her own business (a yoga studio in her home), which is her life's passion.

I was able to take care of my parents, financially, when they fell ill. When my mother was terminally ill, I was able to take her on a trip she had dreamed about, and was also able to pay for my aunt, and my sister to go with her, as they were her care-givers. I love my mom and nothing can replace her. My willingness to go against the grain and fight for what I believed in gave me the most priceless commodity...time with her.

Years later, I watched my dad go through a long debilitating terminal illness. He was a strong, proud, and powerful man. His money had run out, and his ability to work and make more money had run out as well. I was able to lease him a brand new car, and buy his home and give it back to him, so that he could live there for the rest of his life. This allowed him to live his last years with less anxiety and stress, and to eventually die with dignity. Before that though, my financial freedom gave me the ability to make the time to get to really know him and to have his grandchildren get to know him as well. My daughters knew and will always love their grandfather, because of the career choices I made many years ago.

Because of those same choices, I have been able to send my daughters to private schools and private education facilities across North America. I am so proud of them. I mentioned two of them early on in the book, and it's incredible to me how bright, intelligent and dream-focused they are.

Eponine is my oldest, and is bound and determined to become a writer and director in the movie industry.

My middle daughter, Kassidy, is bright, brilliant, and probably the most socially outgoing 17 year old on the planet. Her dreams have no limits, at least in part because of everything she has seen her dad accomplish in building a legacy.

Hailee, my 15 year old, is blessed with the gift of unfaltering commitment. She's an honor roll student, and has been for many years, in one of the toughest private schools in North America. She dances competitively, 20 to 30 hours per week, while maintaining her grades. She has incredible dreams of one day opening a clinic to help people with emotional or mental disorders.

Finally, there's Sydney. At only three years old, she is my youngest and only time will tell what her ambitions will be. Our children will become *not* what we say, but what we will do. Don't underestimate the influence you have over your children. We can only be the best possible examples of the qualities we would like to see in them.

Over the past decade and a half, I have been privileged to give back in many ways. Let me share a couple of examples, just to illustrate the true blessing financial freedom can give you.

There was a young boy in our community, less than 10 years old, who was dying of a brain tumor. His dying wish was to have a trailer up north to stay in, for his last summer, with his sister and his parents. My associates and I set out to raise the money to make this happen for him. Although our fund-raising efforts fell $10,000 short, I was able to write a cheque for the difference instead of having to break the bad news to his family.

For a number of years on Christmas Eve, I got to visit families that had no money for gifts or groceries, and deliver Christmas to them, in the form of a basket of groceries, gifts for each child, a gift for the husband and wife. I remember one family in particular who were about to lose their home due to arrears on their mortgage. I was able to catch up their mortgage as part of my Christmas gift to them. I can't tell you how incredible it felt being able to make such a difference in their lives.

The financial successes I've achieved have given me so many amazing opportunities to help my friends, family, and community, and all because I made a decision with a commitment.

So now you have this incredible business opportunity. All these possibilities and benefits and many more, which I did not have the space to share with you, could be yours. The second you sign up to be an independent businessperson, the doors of opportunity open up for you. I know this from first-hand experience. I have only a grade 10 education, was born into a pretty average and ordinary family, and often struggled with my weight and self-esteem. I just knew I wanted to make a difference, and knew that I only needed an opportunity to make that happen.

"What is your why?"

This is a question often asked in this business. If you have not been asked this yet by your upline/leader, be patient. You will be. Your "why" is your reason for starting your business, your reason for sticking to your commitment when you do not want to, your reason for being a person of your word and maintaining the disciplines that will eventually allow you to be free. Your "why" can be anything that motivates you to get uncomfortable, to make the phone calls necessary to build a business, to explain your company and its products and services to a stranger … anything that motivates you to get the job done.

More often than not, people say their children are their motive. I challenge this. If it is really your children, then why haven't you done anything up to this point? I will tell you why. Frankly, I do not like the idea of a single "why" that can drive you to success. There will not be only one reason that will move you to face the obstacles, hurdles, and negative feedback you might experience on your journey. However, you may be motivated and inspired by the collective goals, dreams, and ambitions of yourself and your family, and thereby allow yourself to be moved into action. It is the law of cause and effect. Allow your current circumstances and desire for better to "cause" you into action, to do the uncomfortable and possibly repetitive, knowing that the "effect" is a life of financial freedom, of dreams achieved and goals reached, and a legacy left behind.

I have seen too many people start a business and say all the right things; they look sharp and dress sharp; they talk about their kids or parents or spouse, or paying off their debts or mortgage; however they do absolutely nothing to reach any those goals.

It comes down to one simple formula: a decision with desire, a piece of commitment, and old-fashioned hard work. Don't be fooled, you can read all the books on purpose and finding your "why", but it is your ability to use that information and knowledge that will cause your life to change. It's been said that 'knowledge is power'. Perhaps the better way of saying it would be *applied knowledge is power*. Get out there and start applying it.

The opportunity that you have before you will require your time and energy. I don't mind telling you that building my business was the toughest thing I've ever done. Having said that, I do not know of any easier way I could have taken my income to $90,000 per month and gained wealth in the process. It is the road to your new life. In this new career—this new life—for the first three to twelve months you'll get to become a dreamer. Then you get to become a dream giver for the next 12 to 60 months as you share your vision with your team and new people. Finally, you'll then get to live that dream for a lifetime.

Life will give you what you are willing to fight for. I am just like you. I've had challenges and obstacles to overcome. I was the chubby kid in the school parking lot who the other kids made fun of. I was the deluded kid who really thought he was going to be a rock star. Then suddenly, like the rest of us, I woke up with a family of my own, a mortgage and responsibility, and was imprisoned by the middle-class way of thinking.

I remember buying my first home in 1991, and saying to the bank manager that I would stay there for the rest of my life—in a 1,600 square-foot home on a crescent, where all the homes were so close together you could barely walk between them. At 25, I had already given up.

Imagine how differently my children would think today, if I had stayed the person I was at 25. Now think about all of the families I have affected in a positive way due to my willingness to suck up my fear, my low self-esteem, and my infinite capacity for feeling sorry for myself, and put it all aside for the greater good.

With clarity, I see today that people are too busy "life-ing" to ever know what it's like to be living. Start living today. Start the incredible journey of overcoming obstacles and opposition, exercise infinite patience, and enjoy freedom and giving. Today your life starts. You are finally free. However, always remember: freedom isn't free. There's a price to be paid for greatness. Don't give up; never give in.

I once heard the following sentence: "I would rather die fighting on my knees than to live standing in chains." Fight. If you fall to your knees, get back up. Pain is inevitable, suffering is an option. Feel the pain; accept the pain, and move on to greatness. Be the person you would want yourself to be if you were watching yourself in a movie.

Thank you for allowing me to share some of the core insights that have allowed the wonderful gifts listed above. I humbly share them with you. I live by the phrase: "much is given, much is expected". So let this book, and some of its small stories, change the course of your journey. Destiny is a design we create in our mind. Redesign your destiny. I look forward to hearing of all your wonderful successes.

May your heart be open, your dreams abundant, and your willingness to give endless.

Raymond Young

After going through a divorce and trying financial times, Raymond Young went on to build one of the largest network marketing businesses in North America. His thirty-year career has been focused on training, developing, and mentoring individuals. He is responsible for inspiring thousands of people through conferences, seminars, and public speaking engagements.

For more information on this book, or to schedule Raymond for a speaking engagement, please call 1-866-885-2760 or email info@werleadership.com

Printed in Canada